T0277436

First Keep God First And All Things Possible...

This Book Is Dedicated to Grandmother Miss Hattie Hancock,

The Founder Of Miss Hattie Southern Cafe and Catering.

Celebrity Executive Chef Of Miss Hattie's

Southern Cafe and Catering Jamon Q Hancock. Graduate of Le Cordon Bleu

MEET MY FAMILY…..

THE HANCOCK'S

Mr. John Hancock

Mrs.Hattie Hancock

My Queen of My Life
My Mommy

Brenda Hancock

(You can see more of my family, friends, and Celebrity friends thought out this cook book)

CHICK PEA SOUP

INGREDIENTS

- 3 tablespoon olive oil
- 1 sweet onion, diced
- 3 garlic cloves, minced
- sea salt and pepper
- 1 teaspoon of rosemary
- 2 can chickpeas, drained and rinsed
- 1 red bell pepper medium dice
- 1 yellow bell pepper medium dice
- 4 cups chicken or vegetable stock
- ¾ cup broccoli
- 1 cup of kale
- 1 cup of carrots
- 5 ounces frozen spinach or 8 ounces fresh spinach
- lemon wedges, for spritzing

Directions

- Heat the olive oil in a large pot over medium-low heat. Stir in the onion and garlic with a big pinch of salt and pepper. Cook for 5 minutes, until translucent. Stir in the rosemary.
- Stir in the chickpeas, chicken vegetable and stock. Bring the mixture to a boil. Once boiling, add in your pasta. Cook until the pasta is al dente. This will be determined on the box of pasta you use, somewhere between 8 and 12 minutes.
- Once the pasta is cooked, stir in the spinach. Taste and season with extra salt and pepper. Ladle into bowls and serve with a lemon wedge for spritzing.

Miss Hattie Homemade Philadelphia Cream Cheese Pound Cake with Candied Pecans

INGREDIENTS

- 3/4 lb. butter
  1/2 (8 ounce) package Philadelphia Cream Cheese
  3 1/2 cups sugar
- 6 eggs
  3 cups cake flour
  1 teaspoon vanilla flavoring
- 2 teaspoon of butter extract
- 1 teaspoon of fresh lemon juice
- 3 teaspoon of white wine of your choice
- 1/4 cup of Eagle Brand Sweetened Condensed Milk

DIRECTIONS

- Note: 3 sticks of butter equal 3/4 lb.
- All ingredients (including eggs and cream cheese) must be at room temperature.
- Cream butter well, add cream cheese.
- Mix thoroughly.
- Gradually add sugar.
- Add eggs, one at a time.
- Add flour gradually, then add vanilla flavor, butter extract, white wine, fresh lemon juice, milk .
- Place cake in tube pan in COLD oven.
- Bake at 325 degrees F (163 degrees C) for 1 1/2 hours (gas oven 1 hour)[from the time you turn on the oven].
- Note: The longer the cream cheese, butter, and eggs sit at room temperature, the better the cake (ingredients can be left out over night).

Cream Cheese Icing

8 ounces cream cheese, at room temperature
1 stick unsalted butter, at room temperature
2 teaspoons vanilla paste (or extract)
2 teaspoons butter extract
3 teaspoon of fresh lemon squeeze
3 cups powdered sugar, sifted (don't skip sifting!)
3 teaspoon of Eagle Brand Sweetened Condensed Milk

Directions
In the bowl of a stand mixer fitted with the paddle attachment, beat the cream cheese, butter, and vanilla and butter extract, lemon, milk on medium-high speed until very light, creamy, and smooth. On low speed, gradually add in the sugar and beat until fluffy. If you need a stiffer consistency for decorative piping, add more powdered sugar.

Candy Pecans

7 tablespoons brown sugar
1 1/2 teaspoons ground cinnamon
1/2 teaspoon fine sea salt
Pinch nutmeg
1/2 teaspoon vanilla extract
1 1/2 tablespoons water
1/2 teaspoon of white wine
2 teaspoons butter extract
3 cups (6 ounces) pecan halves
1/2 stick of salt butter

DIRECTIONS
Line a baking sheet with parchment paper or a silicone baking mat.
Add brown sugar and butter, cinnamon, salt, nutmeg, vanilla, water, white wine, and the butter extract to a medium skillet. Place the skillet over medium heat and cook, stirring often until the brown sugar melts into a bubbling sauce, about 1 minute.
Stir in the pecans so that the brown sugar sauce coats them. Cook, stirring the entire time, until the pecans look candied and smell nutty, 2 to 3 minutes. As the nuts heat up in the pan, the sauce will slowly coat them and become shiny. Watch closely as the nuts cook so that they do not burn.
Transfer the candied pecans to the prepared baking sheet and spread into one layer. Allow the pecans to cool down, and then break them up before serving.
Store cooled candied nuts in an airtight container. They will last at room temperature for one week, in the refrigerator for a few weeks and in the freezer for a month, if not longer.

Miss Hattie Southern Fried Chicken

Ingredients

- 4 cups all-purpose flour, divided
- 2 tablespoons garlic salt
- 1 tablespoon chili powder
- 3 teaspoons pepper, divided
- 2-1/2 teaspoons poultry seasoning
- 2 large eggs
- 1-1/2 cups milk
- 1 teaspoon sea salt
- 2 broiler/fryer chickens (3-1/2 to 4 pounds each), cut up
- Oil for deep-fat frying

Directions

1. In a large shallow dish, combine 2-2/3 cups flour, garlic salt, chili powder, 2-1/2 teaspoons pepper and poultry seasoning. In another shallow dish, beat eggs and 1-1/2 cups milk ; add sea salt and the remaining 1-1/3 cups flour and 1/2 teaspoon pepper. Dip chicken in egg mixture, then place in flour mixture, a few pieces at a time. Turn to coat.
2. In a deep-fat fryer, heat oil to 375°. Fry chicken, several pieces at a time, until chicken is golden brown and juices run clear, 7-8 minutes on each side. Drain on paper towels.

Chef Hancock Homemade Peach and Apple Cobbler

Ingredients

1 cup of pancake mix
6   peaches
6 granny smith apples
2 cup of sugar
1 cup of brown sugar
1 1/2 tablespoons of cinnamon
3 tablespoons red wine of your choice
1 14 oz of milk eagle brand sweetened condensed milk
1 tablespoon of butter extract
2 tablespoons of vanilla extract
1 teaspoon of almond extract
1/3 cup of Butter pancake syrup

Directions

1/3 Melt butter and pour into 9×13 baking dish. Mix pancake   batter and pour over butter evenly. Now for the pancake batter mix milk almond extract, butter extract and mix. Cook granny smith apple and peaches with butter, sugar, wine, pancake syrup, vanilla extract for 15 mins in a medium pot. Pour off peaches and granny smith apple in pan with butter and pour the pancake batter on top. Sprinkle with pinch or 2 of brown sugar and cinnamon. Bake for 40 minutes. Perfect!

Chef Hancock Southern Style Homemade Green Beans

Ingredients

3 pounds of fresh green beans
2 tablespoon sea salt (add more if needed)
2 tablespoon season salt (add more if needed)
2 teaspoon rosemary
3 tablespoon black pepper (add more if needed)
2 tablespoon chili power
6 your choice of smoke turkey parts or pork
6 red potatoes
1 red onion medium dice
3 tablespoons minced garlic
3 tablespoons liquid smoke
3 tablespoons hot sauce
32 oz of vegetables stock
2 tablespoons soy sauce
1 red bell pepper small dice
1 yellow bell pepper small dice
1/3 cup of white wine of your choice
1/4 of vegetables oil

Directions

Start off by placing the smoked turkey into a large pot.
Pour the vegetable stock, black pepper, sea salt, season salt, minced garlic ,hot sauce, all the pepper remand yellow, vegetable oil, soy sauce, liquid smoke, onions, chili power, rose marry,and wine then turn the heat to high.
Let the turkey cook until it's nice and tender, then remove it from the pot. Be sure to NOT drain the liquid from the pot. We will use it!
Shred or dice up the turkey meat. Make sure to remove all the bones, and skin.
Now toss the green beans, smoked turkey pot with the liquid.
Sprinkle in the seasonings, and stir the ingredients.
Cook for about 10 minutes, then add in the potatoes.
Cook until everything is nice and tender, or cook to your preference.

Miss Hattie Slow Cook Pot Roast

Ingredients

4-5 pound chuck roast
2 tablespoons vegetable oil
2 teaspoons sea salt
4 teaspoon coarse ground black pepper
2 teaspoon rosemary
1 pound carrots peeled and cut into 2" chunks
2 pounds red potatoes and cut into large chunks
2 cloves garlic minced
1 large yellow onion
1 green bell pepper medium dice
1 red bell pepper medium dice
1 32 oz beef broth
2 tablespoons corn starch
3 tablespoons red wine of your choice
minced parsley optional, for garnish

Instructions

- Season the chuck roast with the sea salt, pepper, rosemary and if you would like to , adjust to your taste or you can even leave the salt out altogether since you're adding broth).
- Heat your pan (or if you can brown in your slow cooker, do it in that insert to medium high.
- Add the canola oil and when it ripples and is hot add in the roast and brown, deeply, for 4-5 minutes on each side.
- In your slow cooker add the and wine , carrots, potatoes red and green bell pepper with onions and garlic.
- Lay the beef on top, then add the beef broth and cover, cooking on low for 8-10 hours or on high for 5-6 hours.
- In the last hour mix your cornstarch and water and add it to the slow cooker to thicken the sauce or you can take the food out when done cooking, and add the leftover liquid to a small saucepan with the cornstarch/water mixture and cook on high for just 2-3 minutes until the liquid is thickened into a gravy.
- Pour the gravy over the meat and garnish with parsley if desired.

Deep Fried Cauliflower

Prep 10 minutes Cook 20 minutesTotal 30 minutes

Ingredients

1 head cauliflower (cut into small pieces)
1 beksul frying mix for cooking
1 teaspoon Garlic powder
1 teaspoon of black pepper
½ teaspoon sea salt
1 cup milk
1 egg
1 tablespoon Chili powder
Vegetable oil for frying

Instructions

- In a large bowl mix , egg, pepper, chili powder, garlic power and salt. Add milk, beksul frying mix for cooking, sauce and mix until the batter is smooth.
- Dip cauliflower pieces into the batter and coat evenly. Allow excess batter to drip off.
- Repeat until all cauliflower pieces are coated.
- Heat deep fryer to 365 degrees. Deep fry cauliflower pieces in batches until golden brown. Drain on paper towels.

Nice And Refreshing Strawberry And Fried Goat Cheese With Pecans with and Balsamic Dressing Salad

Ingredients:

Salad

- 6-ounce log of goat cheese, sliced into 8 pieces
- ¼ cup all-purpose flour
- 2 large egg, lightly beaten
- ½ cup panko breadcrumbs
- Oil, for frying
- 5 ounces arugula (or spring mix and kale)
- 6 ounces strawberries, trimmed and quartered
- 1 cup whole pecans
- 1 small avocado, sliced
- 2 Persian cucumbers, sliced

Balsamic Dressing

- ¼ cup olive oil
- 2 tablespoons balsamic vinegar
- 1 tablespoon honey
- 1 ½ teaspoons Dijon mustard
- ¼ teaspoon sea salt
- 1 tablespoon of black pepper
- 1 teaspoon rosemary
- 1 teaspoon of brown sugar

Instructions

- **DREDGE:** Place the flour and ¼ teaspoon salt in a small shallow bowl; whisk. Add beaten egg and panko in two more shallow bowls. Dip the goat cheese slice in the flour, then egg mixture, and finally, panko. Place on a plate. Repeat this with the remaining goat cheese.
- **FRY:** Heat a frying pan over medium heat with ½ cup of frying oil. When the oil is hot, add the goat cheese medallions in a single layer and pan for 3-4 minutes, flipping halfway. Remove to a paper towel-lined plate.
- **DRESSING:** Add the ingredients to a mason jar and shake well to combine. If dressing separates before dressing salad, re-shake jar.
- **SALAD:** Place arugula in a large salad bowl, add strawberries, pecans, avocado, and cucumbers. Toss the salad with half of the balsamic dressing, adjust as needed. Then serve topped with goat cheese medallions

GRILLED CHICKEN AND VEGETABLES

Ingredients

For the marinade
- ¼ cup olive oil
- ¼ cup fresh lemon juice
- 4 garlic cloves crushed
- 1 tsp smoked paprika
- ½ tsp chili power
- 1 tsp dried oregano
- 1 tsp sea salt
- black pepper to taste

For grilling
- 4 large chicken breasts skinless + de-boned
- 2 bell peppers seeds removed and sliced into thick strips
- broccolini
- 12-16 spears asparagus woody ends trimmed
- 2-3 large zucchini/courgette sliced into thick slices

Instructions
- Pre-heat the grill/griddle pan.
- Season the chicken with salt and allow to sit while you make the marinade.
- Combine all the marinade ingredients and mix well. Pour half of the marinade over the chicken and the other half over the vegetables. Allow to marinade for a few minutes.
- Grill the chicken for 5-7 minutes per side (depending on thickness) until cooked to your preference. Remove from the grill, cover with foil and allow to rest while you grill the vegetables.
-
- Grill the vegetables until they are starting to char and are cooked to your preference. Remove from the grill and serve with the chicken and lemon wedges for squeezing.

Chef Hancock The Best Collar Greens in the World…..

Ingredients

2 bush of fresh kale
4 bush of fresh collar greens
2 jalapeño small dice with seeds
1 large yellow onion
3 turkey or pork smoke meats of your choice
3 Tablespoons of Liquid smoke
2 tablespoon Sea salt
3 tablespoon Black pepper
2 tablespoon Seasoning salt
3 tablespoons of soy sauce
3 teaspoons of hot sauce
2 32 oz of vegetables stock
1/4 cup vegetable oil

Directions

tart off by placing the smoked turkey into a large pot.
Pour the vegetable stock, black pepper, sea salt, season salt, minced garlic, hot sauce, vegetable oil, jalapeño ,soy sauce, liquid smoke, onions, chili power, rosemarry ,and wine then turn the heat to high.
Let the turkey cook until it's nice and tender, then remove it from the pot. Be sure to NOT drain the liquid from the pot. We will use it!
Shred or dice up the turkey meat. Make sure to remove all the bones, and skin.
Now toss the kale and collar , smoked turkey pot with the liquid.
Sprinkle in the seasonings, and stir the ingredients.
Cook for about 60 minutes.
Cook until everything is nice and tender, or cook to your preference.

My No Bake No Bake Cheese Cake

Ingredients

12 oz cream cheese softened
2/3 cup sour cream
1 cup powdered sugar
1 teaspoon of vanilla
1 teaspoon of lemon
3 teaspoon of eagle brand condensed milk
5 tablespoon cool whip

1 9 inch graham cracker pie crust

Add fresh fruit on top if you like….

Directions

In a medium bowl, beat cream cheese, sour cream, sugar, vanilla, lemon, milk and cool whip until smooth.
Pour into crust.
Refrigerate for at least 1 1/2 hour.

EKLIPSE TELEVISION NETWORKS PRESENTS:

THE REAL CHEF'S OF
ATLANTA
CASTING CALL....
JUNE 26,2021 @ 10:30 TO 2:30 P.M.
GLENLAKE PKWY NC
ATLANTA,GA 30328
678-387-3509

Roku
Channel

CHEF HANCOCK
EVENT'S

Dress To Impress
"Filming Live" for TV
Thank
You For Your Support.
Ticket # 1

Sip & Taste

A Summer Winedown
By the Pool
This Sunday Oct. 4th 1pm
With this Ticket You will get:
1-Adult Drink
1-Soft Drink
Appetizers By Chef Galexy
A Grilled Surprise By
Chef Hancock &
A Tasty Surprise
By Chef Shy
Taking Donations for:

October
BREST
CANCER

W♥RTH
the Wait

A Sip & Taste Event
Sun, October 4 at 1:00 PM
By Eklipse TV Network

Tickets $25
Seating Is Limited
(213)282-3588

Chef Hancock And Film Producer&Actor Dennis White

Chef Hancock and Celebrity

Backstage in Palm Spring with Legends:ERIC FLOYD,WANDA DEE,DIONNE WARWICK,VIVIAN REED&JAMES LONDON.

Chef H with Atlanta House Wife
Actress Drew Sidora

Chef. Hancock with Jive Records Public
Announcement

Chef H with Young Money Artist Gudda
Gudda (LordGudda)

Chef H with Dj Unk from OOMP
Camp

Chef H with CEO of Hype T.V. and Magazine Jay..

Celebrity Chef Hancock and
Chopped Chef Christine Hazel

Chef H with Artist's Zues and America
Idol DeAndre Perryman

Chef Hancock's Family
& Friends

The Hancock

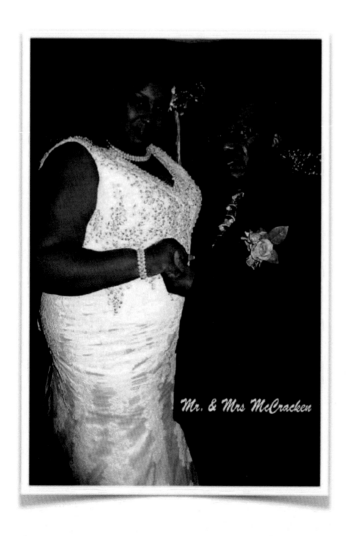

Mr. & Mrs McCracken

Hubby and His Mother

Chef H and My Love of My life
Hubby and our Little King..

Aunt Keshia and chef Hancock

Chef Hancock Famous Salmon Croquettes

Ingredients
SALMON

4 (6 oz each) salmon filets
1/2 tsp sea salt
1/2 tsp black pepper
1/2 tsp smoked paprika (or regular paprika)
1/4 tsp chili power

SAUCE
6 Tbsp butter
2 tsp olive oil
3 cloves garlic *minced*
1/2 cup honey
6 Tbsp white wine of your choice
5 Tbsp liquid smoke
1 Tbsp rosemary
6 Tbsp lemon juice

Instructions
- Pat salmon dry, then season with salt, pepper, paprika and chili power (if using). Set aside. Adjust oven rack to middle position, then preheat broiler.
- Add butter and oil to a large, oven-safe skillet over MED-HIGH heat. Once butter is melted, add garlic, wine, liquid smoke , rosemary, honey and lemon juice and cook 30 seconds or so, until sauce is heated through.
- Add salmon, skin side down (if using salmon with skin), and cook 3 minutes. While salmon cooks, baste frequently with sauce from the pan by spooning it over the top of the salmon.
- Broil salmon for 5-6 minutes, basting with sauce once during the broil, until salmon is caramelized and cooked to desired doneness.
- Garnish with minced parsley if desired.

Lemon Red Snapper with Herbed Butter

Ingredients

- 2 lemons
- 1/2 cup of red wine of your choice
- Cooking spray
- 4 (6-ounce) red snapper
- ¼ teaspoon sea salt
- ¼ teaspoon paprika
- ¼ teaspoon black pepper
- 2 tablespoons butter, softened
- 1 ½ teaspoons chopped fresh herbs (such as rosemary, thyme, basil, or parsley)

Directions

- Step 1 Preheat oven to 425°.
- Step 2 Cut 1 lemon into 8 slices. Place slices, in pairs, on a rimmed baking sheet coated with cooking spray. Grate remaining lemon to get 1 teaspoon lemon rind; set aside. Reserve lemon for another use.
- Step 3 Place 1 fillet on top of each pair of lemon slices. Combine salt, paprika, and pepper; red wine, sprinkle evenly over fish. Bake at 425° for 13 minutes or until fish flakes easily when tested with a fork or until desired degree of doneness.
- Step 4 While fish bakes, combine reserved lemon rind, butter, and herbs in a small bowl.
- Step 5 Place fish and lemon slices on individual serving plates; top each fillet with herbed butter, spreading to melt, if desired. Garnish with herb sprigs, if desired.

Chef Hancock 15 Beans Soup

Ingredients

- 1 package HamBeens® 15 BEAN SOUP®
- 4 Alkaline Water With PH
- 4 cups low sodium chicken broth
- 1 Bush Kale Freash
- 1 onion diced
- 2 cloves garlic minced
- 15 ounces diced tomatoes with juice
- 1 teaspoon chili powder
- 1 teaspoon sea salt
- 2 teaspoon of rosemary
- 1 red bell pepper small dice
- 1 teaspoon black pepper
- 1 tablespoon lemon juice

Directions

- Rinse beans and drain. Sort any unwanted debris .

- Place beans in a large pot of cool water. Cover and allow to soak at least 8 hours or overnight. After soaking, drain water.

- Add water and broth to a large pot.

- Add with the water and broth to a large pot. Bring to a boil, reduce heat to a simmer, and cover. Cook 1 hour.

- Add, onion, garlic, and drained beans and reduce heat to a simmer, and cover. Cook 1 ½ to 2 hours or until beans are tender.

- Stir in tomatoes, chili powder, and lemon juice. Simmer uncovered for an additional 30 minutes or until thickened.

- Stir in the rose marry, kale, bell pepper, from the beans and season with salt & pepper to taste. Simmer 25 minute more.

Chef Hancock Home Made Strawberry Cake

CAKE

Ingredients

- 1 cup white sugar
- ½ cup salted butter
- 2 large eggs
- 2 teaspoons vanilla extract
- 1 ½ cups all-purpose cake flour
- 1 ¾ teaspoons baking powder
- ½ cup milk

Directions

- Preheat the oven to 350 degrees F (175 degrees C). Grease and flour a 9-inch square cake pan.
- Cream sugar and butter together in a mixing bowl. Add eggs, one at a time, beating briefly after each addition. Mix in vanilla.
- Combine cake flour and baking powder in a separate bowl. Add to the wet ingredients and mix well. Add milk and stir until smooth. Pour batter into the prepared cake pan.
- Bake in the preheated oven until the top springs back when lightly touched, 30 to 40 minutes.
- Remove from the oven and cool completely.

STRAWBERRY FILLING

Ingredients

- 1/2 cup of water
- 1/2 cup white wine of your choice
- 3 tablespoons cornstarch
- 1 ½ cups frozen strawberries, thawed and cut into bite size pieces
- 1 cup of fresh strawberries cut in slice small dice
- ¾ cup white sugar

Directions

- Whisk water and cornstarch together in a large saucepan. Stir in strawberries and sugar.

- Cook over medium heat until thickened, about 10 minutes. Allow to cool completely before use.

BUTTER CREAM CHEESE ICING
Ingredients

- 8 ounces cream cheese (1 brick, 226 grams), softened to room temperature
- ½ cup salted butter (1 stick, 113 grams), softened to room temperature
- 4 cups powdered sugar (455 grams), sifted
- 1 teaspoons butter extract
- 1 teaspoon lemon juice
- 2 teaspoons vanilla extract

Instructions

- Beat the cream cheese, butter, powdered sugar, vanilla, butter extract, lemon, with an electric mixer on low until combined.
- Turn speed up to high and beat for 4-5 minutes until smooth, light, and creamy. Stop and scrape down the bowl 1-2 times to make sure it mixing well.

Make ahead: Buttercream can be stored in the fridge for 1 week and in the freezer for at least a month. Let come to room temperature and beat until smooth before using.

The Best Star Fruit Salad

Ingredients

- 1 cantaloupe balls, peeled and cut into bite-sized pieces (use melon baller tool)
- 2 cups green grapes, sliced in half
- 16 ounces strawberries, cut into bite-sized pieces
- 1 pineapple, peeled and cut into bite-sized pieces
- 1 cup black grapes

Honey Lemon Dressing

- 1/2 teaspoon lemon zest
- 3 tablespoons lemon juice
- 1/2 apple juice
- 6 tablespoon honey
- 1 teaspoon cinnamon

Instructions

- Combine all the prepared fruit in a large glass bowl.
- Combine lemon zest, lemon juice apple juice, cinnamon, and honey in a small bowl or souted cup. Mix well
- Pour the honey lime dressing over the fruit and gently stir to combine. Serve and enjoy!

Chef Hancock Designer Chocolate Chip Cookies

Ingredients

- 1 cup butter, softened
- 1 cup white sugar
- 1 cup packed brown sugar
- 2 eggs
- 2 teaspoons vanilla extract
- 1 teaspoon baking soda
- 2 teaspoons milk
- ½ teaspoon salt
- 3 cups all-purpose flour
- 2 cups semisweet chocolate chips
- 1 cup chopped pecan
- 1/2 cup of caramel sauce for garnish

Directions

1. Gather your ingredients, making sure your butter is softened, and your eggs are room temperature.
2. Preheat the oven to 350 degrees F (175 degrees C).
3. Beat butter, white sugar, and brown sugar with an electric mixer in a large bowl until smooth.
4. Beat in eggs, one at a time, then stir in vanilla.
5. Dissolve baking soda in hot water. Add to batter along with salt.
6. Stir in flour, chocolate chips, and pecan.
7. Drop spoonfuls of dough two inches apart onto un-greased baking sheets.

Hire Us for you next event…

Showing Bussiness Love

Chef Hancock Lemon Pepper Wings

Xzavion Curry Baseball 71
Guardians and Chef Hancock

Chef Hancock At GT

Coming Soon Summer 2024....

Download App:

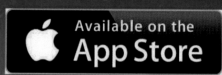

www.eklipseworldwide.com

SHOWING LOVE TO BUSNIESS

A vitamin store and juice bar featuring fresh, all-natural, all-organic juices, smoothies, and protein shakes.

4450 NELSON BRONGDON BLVD STE C-6

SUGAR HILL,Ga 30518

678-824-3071

Danielle L. Brison
Future Director
314-365-8961
Iamtuppenough@gmail.com
www.my.tupperware.com/cannabeebee
Join us on Facebook
@CannaBeeBeeShareTupperware

Where WILL
THE party
TAKE YOU?
Tupperware

Change Your Coffee, Change Your Life!
PAT PURLEY
Independent Distributor
(314) 306-9017
Email: jc1177pap@yahoo.com
blessyourhealth.info

ORGANO

blessyourhealth.myorganogold.com

"Beloved, I wish above all things thou mayest prosper and be in health, even asthy soul prospereth." (3 John 1:2 KJV)

TO ORDER OR BECOME A DISTRIBUTOR
1-877-674-2661
Dis #10001891093

Miss Hattie Famous
"Gand Ma Ma Punch"

LEMON JUICE
PINAPPLE JUICE
STRAWBERRY
SUGAR
ORANGE
BLUE BERRY
PINEAPPLE
ALKALINE WATER
HONEY
CINNAMON
APPLE JUICE 100%

Put all in a punch bowl and mix
together....Knock yourself out....

THE FABULOUS FLOYDS'
FRUIT SOUP

FRESH SLICES OF….
GRAPES
CHERRY
BANANA
PINEAPPLE
BLUEBERRY
STRAWBERRY

THEN ADD
HONEY
CINNAMON

SQUEEZE SOME..
LIME
LEMON

POUR IN..
100% PINEAPPLE JUICE
100% CRANBERRY JUICE

Chef Hancock And My Executive
Assistant Jay

The Real Chef's of Atlanta Coming Soon...

Celebrity Chef Hancock and Actress
and Comedian Roz Ryan from TV
show Amen.

Check out Neo Soul Artist:

Aysia BerLynn

www.aysiaberlynn.com